The Science of Starting Over

How to Let Go of the Past, Turn Your Pain into Strength, and Rebuild Your Life from Scratch

By Hung Pham
http://www.missionandpossible.com

Your Free Gift

As a way of showing my gratitude, I'm offering a resource that's exclusive only to you.

[>> CLICK HERE for your FREE eBook on the 5 Key Strategies I Used to Turn My Life Around](#)

It's tough not to feel lost in life. The secret is to find out what changes are needed and how to make those changes. In my free eBook, I'll show how to:

- Remove self-limiting beliefs using this one simple trick
- Stop worrying about future so that you can focus on the present
- Find the best advice on what to do in your current situation

- Stop living in the past and how to start moving forward
- Appreciate your life more by reframing your thinking
- And much more

>> CLICK HERE to download your FREE eBook now!

Table of Contents

THE SCIENCE OF STARTING OVER: HOW TO LET GO OF THE PAST, TURN YOUR PAIN INTO STRENGTH, REBUILD YOUR LIFE FROM SCRATCH

TABLE OF CONTENTS 4

INTRODUCTION 7

LETTING GO OF THE PAST 13

HOW IT ALL STARTED 14

#1 DON'T WORRY, EVERYBODY FAILS 20

#2 CHANGE AN OUTCOME BY CHANGING YOUR PERSPECTIVE 26

#3 LIVE LIFE WITH RESULTS NOT REGRETS 31

#4 CATS AREN'T THE ONLY ONES WITH NINE LIVES 37

DEPRESSION, ADDICTION, AND HOW MY 20'S WERE A BLUR 40

#5 STOP VICTIMIZING YOURSELF, STOP BLAMING OTHERS 48

#6 MAKE THE MOST OF THE TIME YOU HAVE NOW 51

EMBRACE YOUR MISTAKES............................55

WHEN LIFE GIVES YOU LEMONS, GRAB SOME SALT AND TEQUILA..56

#7 STOP MAKING PROBLEMS BIGGER THAN THEY ARE..63

#8 BE TRUE TO YOURSELF AND OWN WHO YOU ARE..69

#9 USE YOUR STORY TO INSPIRE OTHERS 73

#10 HAPPINESS ON THE INSIDE EQUALS HAPPINESS ON THE OUTSIDE 76

MAKING YOUR COMEBACK 81

WHEN YOU'RE GOING THROUGH HELL, KEEP GOING..82

#11 START SMALL, START NOW 86

#12 CHANGE YOUR ENVIRONMENT TO CHANGE YOUR LIFE 92

#13 HOW A FOUR-LETTER WORD CAN SPARK CHANGE 98

#14 KEEP ONE EYE ON THE PAST AND ONE ON THE FUTURE 102

#15 INVEST IN YOURSELF FOR THE GREATEST RETURN POSSIBLE 105

#16 CREATING A BLUEPRINT FOR SUCCESS .110

#17 HOW TO BEGIN TODAY 114

CONCLUSION 117

CHEAT SHEET 120

ABOUT THE AUTHOR 125

Introduction

I almost didn't write this book. In fact, every time I opened up a document and started to type, I would click the X in the top right corner and close without saving. I knew that by writing this book, it would force me to relive parts of my past that conjure up feelings of sadness and pain.

It would also force me to put those painful parts out in the open, even though I had buried them away for years. But I knew that if I wrote this book, it would help many people who are in the same or similar situation I was in years ago.

That's why I'm writing this book.

Because it's not about me anymore, I'm no longer trying to victimize myself. It's about you, the problems you're facing, and how this book can help turn your life around. It's about getting better and feeling better every day. If there's anything that I believe strongly in, it's that everyone has a right to be happy.

Everyone has a right to live the life they want to live.

In all my books I always include a few personal stories to reinforce the point I'm making. However, in this book, you'll get to read even more personal stories that are very near and dear to my heart. The fact that I can share it with you is a testament to how far I've come and grown.

I hope one day I can read one of your stories too. That way I'll know you're in a much better place.

The techniques in this book fall into one of these three broad categories:

- **Letting Go of The Past:** Helping you move on from any mistakes, regrets, or unwanted feelings you may still be internalizing.

- **Embracing Who You Are:** Helping you come to terms with who you are, loving yourself, and being happier overall.

- **Turning Your Life Around:** Focusing on the changes and actions you need to make.

Like I said before, everyone has a right to live the life they want to live. It doesn't matter what kind of upbringing you had or where you are in life today. If you are determined to get better, then this book is for you.

I'm not an expert or claim to be one. I don't have advanced degrees in psychology, psychiatry, or anything behavioral. What makes me capable of writing this book is that I'm a regular person who's made his share of mistakes in life.

I used to wake up every morning wishing my crappy life was just a dream. I used to drive to work and hope a random car would run me off the world. Most importantly, I've got a message for you.

You can always start over no matter how bad it seems

I used to hate motivational quotes with a passion. Every time I read one, I thought to myself, *"How could anyone suffering read a quote like 'Don't Worry, Be Happy' and expect things to get better magically?"*

Motivational quotes felt like a sham to me. Were manufactured like fortune cookies; being made in volume with no real substance or meaning behind them?

It wasn't until I started turning my life around that I came to appreciate motivational quotes. When people began to ask me for advice, I noticed some of my advice sounded a lot like motivational quotes. I would say things like:

"All the things you want in life are outside of your comfort zone."

"As long as you keep moving, you'll eventually get there."

And my favorite

"Until you learn how to fail, you won't fully succeed."

Wait a minute, was I being hypocritical? How could the guy who hated motivational quotes now give them as advice? Then it dawned on me. Motivation quotes are born from pain and suffering. They represented the struggle that comes with progression.

When I was at my lowest, it was hard for me to understand the quotes because I hadn't progressed yet. I was still suffering. It wasn't until I dug myself out of the hole that I understood why they exist.

Making mistakes is human. Some mistakes are bigger than others, but at the end of the day, we all make them. It's also human to have compassion and help those who have made the same mistakes we have. From that cycle of struggle and progress, motivational quotes are born.

Because of this, I'm going to start each section with one of my favorite motivational quotes. Now if you don't believe in them like how I once was, give me a chance. By the end of this book, I guarantee that you'll look at life through a much brighter lens.

I know it's tough right now, but trust me life is worth living. I promise.

Letting Go of the Past

"When I let go of what I am, I become what I might be" – Lao Tzu

How It All Started

Growing up, my dad pushed me hard academically. I guess you can say I had the prototypical Asian parents; you know the ones that don't accept anything less than straight A's. Because of this, I struggled with finding my identity at a young age. Everything I did was to make my parents happy. I put their happiness before mine.

As a child, I did whatever my parents asked me to. I spent most of my summers studying, while my friends were out and about. I even played the piano for six years and hated every bit of it. However, once I hit puberty, I began to rebel just like any other adolescent.

Being a teenager and fighting against my parents was always a losing battle since I depended on them for everything. Instead, I learned to work within the system they created. Because they both worked and weren't around to monitor me, my grades were a priority for them.

I figured that if I consistently got good grades, they would ease up and allow me more freedom to be a teenager. And that's exactly what I did. Starting with middle school and going all the way to my junior year in high school I got straight A's every report card. My dad was extremely proud.

Like I had expected, my parents began giving me more freedom. I was active in school clubs, became involved in student council, and even joined the wrestling team. I attended lots of school functions, stayed out late at times, and even went out on the weekends. I also abused my freedom because going out and staying out late wasn't always school related.

My parents didn't seem to mind because all that mattered were my grades. As long as my grades were good, everything else was an afterthought. Getting good grades became easy, almost too easy. Entering my senior year, I was in the top two percent of my class.

My senior year proved to be a different story. The summer before my senior year, my girlfriend broke up with me. She was my first love, and we were together for two years up until that point. She told me she needed space but a week after we broke up I saw her attending the homecoming dance with another guy.

I was devastated. My senior year was one of the worst years of my life. For the entire school year, I drove off campus to eat lunch because being in school was too depressing. I could never stay focused in class. That year I got my first C ever and didn't even go to my senior prom.

When it came time for college applications, I barely even applied to any schools. Because of the mental and emotional state I was in, I was scared to leave home for college. That's how much of an emotional wreck I was.

Instead, I applied to a local college so I could stay close to home and be near my family. I convinced myself that this was a good decision because it would be less of a financial burden on my parents but deep down I didn't want to go there.

I dreaded the first day of college. I felt like I should have been at a better university yet I wasn't. I kept asking myself, what was the whole point of doing so well in high school if I was going to end up at a state university? I couldn't accept being there.

That semester I got a 1.8 GPA. I was also put on academic probation and required to get counseling or risk getting kicked out of school. I lost any drive I had for academics; I was mentally checked out.

Until that point, I never experienced failure before. The closest I got to failure was maybe an A minus on a report card.

To go from being a top student to almost getting kicked out of college was too much for me to handle. I needed help, and fast.

I turned to the only person who I thought could help me, the man who pushed me hard academically, my dad. My dad and I never talked much growing up. He was always busy working, and as long as my grades were good, he didn't worry much.

This conversation would be different. For the first time in his life, my dad would see his son in a different light. My dad worked long hours; sometimes 10 – 12 hour days. Because of this, he usually went to bed right after dinner. On this night, though, he stayed up with me.

I was scared to tell him what happened but I knew if anyone could help me it was him. So I nervously told him about everything that was going on in my life and school. These were the first words out of his mouth.

"All these years I thought you were special and now I realize you're not."

To be eighteen-years-old and hear this from your father was one of the most heart-breaking experiences in my life. After listening to that, my brain went numb. I don't recall the rest of the conversation. I just remember bits and pieces of how my dad said I was mentally weak and needed to be a man.

If I was going to succeed, I had to do it for myself. I couldn't rely on my dad anymore. That's the mentality I took with me going forward. As much as it hurt and bothered me, I used it as motivation to drive me towards success.

However, my relationship with my dad would never be the same. I would spend the next fifteen years hardly speaking to him because I resented him for what he said to me that night. I hated him for not being there when I needed him most. I blamed him for all my struggles.

The reality though was that I was a coward and couldn't accept my own failures. I needed to blame others to make myself feel better. I was only able to move forward once I learned to let things go.

#1 Don't Worry, Everybody Fails

In January 2015, an article was making its way around the Internet about a thirty-year-old handsome socialite named Thomas Gilbert Jr., who shot and killed his father. Gilbert Jr. was a Princeton graduate and son of a wealthy millionaire hedge fund manager.

An argument ensued because Gilbert's dad had cut his allowance from $600/month to $400/month and threatened to stop paying his monthly apartment rent of $2400. My initial reaction when I read this article was *"What the heck?"*

Here was a guy who grew up with the best things in life that money could buy. He had a great education and never had to worry about being homeless. Yet, to kill his dad over $200 a month left me completely baffled.

But his story isn't uncommon. I've also read about athletes who made millions in their career and are now broke. Some even end up in prison for committing fraud. I'm not talking about athletes nobody has ever heard of. These are guys who made millions in their playing career.

How can you be completely broke after making tens of millions of dollars in your career?

How can you justify killing your own father over a $200 dispute? Especially when you come from such a wealthy family?

These are just two stories among others where people with such a privileged life squander it away. Regardless of how great somebody's life may seem on the surface it doesn't tell the entire story.

Let me explain a bit more.

When I was struggling to land a job, I had moments where I thought to myself, *"What if I had gone to a better college instead? How would my life have changed?"* I know it sounds dumb but I believed that the college I graduated from held me back.

I felt like there was a stigma towards people who didn't come from known universities. I always felt like the college that I graduated from wasn't a fair representation of talent. Everyone knows what graduating from Stanford or Harvard means. Nobody cares if you graduated from San Jose State.

It would be something that I would struggle with for many years.

I couldn't change where I had gone to school but I can change how I felt about it. I could change how I approached life going forward. During my last two years in school, I hustled my butt off to get internships at two of the top tech companies in the world, Cisco and Sun Microsystems.

I did this because I wanted a strong resume for myself upon graduating. I wanted that edge over others in the job market. Most importantly, I wanted to prove to myself that I didn't need to come from a known university to work at a top tier tech company. After graduation I was offered a full time job at Sun Microsystems.

When you're struggling, it's easy to say, *"Well life would be much easier if I were a millionaire"*. But having money or status doesn't guarantee you anything in life. It makes life a bit easier but there's no promise you'll be happy.

If there's anything I want you to take-away from this chapter, it's the following:

- Failure can come in many forms; failed marriages, failed businesses, failed relationships, failed jobs etc., nobody is immune to this.

- Fame and fortune does not guarantee success. Lots of people have fame and fortune and are still miserable.

- Look at all the greatest people in history and the adversity they overcame to get to where they are. Greatness never came to anyone without failure and struggle.

- It's okay to fail but it is never okay to give up. So don't give up.

#2 Change an Outcome by Changing Your Perspective

One of my favorite quotes of all time is:

"Change the things you can't accept and accept the things you can't change."

In other words, if you're going to complain then do something about it, otherwise stop complaining. Everybody has that one friend who's always complaining about something. It's like the world was specifically making their life harder.

Or so they think.

The truth is everybody has problems. No matter how hard you think your life is, there's always someone out there who has it just as bad, or worse. In fact, there are people right now that are getting by with much less than what you and I have.

If you grew up poor, you can't change that. If you grew up with divorced parents, there's nothing you can do about it. It's always easy to blame all your problems on somebody, or something else.

What happens if all you do is blame your failures on others? What happens to these so-called problems you have in your life? They don't go anywhere. Blaming others for your shortcomings doesn't solve anything.

All you did was direct the attention away from the root of your problems. I believe that everything starts and ends with you. I get it, life isn't fair, and it may never be fair. Someone out there will always be taller, smarter, or richer than the both of us. It's out of our control.

However, the only way your life changes for the better is when you start changing the way you look at life.

I resented my dad so much, that for fifteen years we hardly talked. Because I couldn't get my act together, I always blamed him for not being supportive, not loving me, and not being there when I needed him most.

Now that I'm older and wiser, I couldn't be any more wrong. I was immature, selfish, and always victimized myself. My parents immigrated here from Vietnam right at the end of the war to give my siblings and I a better life.

My dad worked several jobs so that we could have a roof over our heads and food on the table. Even though he couldn't be there all the time for us, he did his best to make sure we had every opportunity to succeed.

Rather than see all the sacrifices he made for us, all I saw was what he said that had upset me. As a result, I created this rift between us for fifteen years. It didn't help that I never talked to him about the problem. My dad just assumed that I didn't care to talk to him anymore.

I couldn't let go of my anger and my pride. Maybe I should've put myself in his shoes and saw things from his perspective. Maybe it was tough for him to see his son fail. All I thought about was how I felt. Whatever the case, I let my pride get the better of me and refused to speak to him for fifteen years.

Sometimes I wonder how things would've been different had I not been so resentful. Maybe I wouldn't have kept making mistakes in life. Maybe if he saw that his perfect son wasn't perfect and hurting inside, it would've brought us closer together.

These days the relationship between my dad and I are getting better. I'm still working on opening-up more especially since he's getting older. All I can do now is make the most of the time we have left together.

Part of learning to let go is to change how you look at things. That's the power of perspective. When an incident has happened, you control how it affects you. You determine how you let it influence your life. That's how you create change.

#3 Live Life with Results Not Regrets

I hate regret. I used to live with lots of regrets, and it held me back for years. Every time something didn't go my way, I would think "if only I had done this," or "if I had made a difference choice instead." I was always dwelling on the negative, and it drove me crazy because I couldn't move on.

Remember the story earlier when I got a 1.8 GPA my first semester of school and was on academic probation?

From day one, I couldn't accept the fact that I was at a local state university. Because of this, I wasn't able to focus and had no desire to do well in school. Every day I would ask myself questions like, *"what am I doing here?"* and *"how is this even possible?"*

I avoided all contact with my friends from high school because I didn't want anyone to know where I went to college. I was embarrassed, especially since many of my high school peers expected me to go to a well-known university. This caused me to lose touch with so many friends.

Because I lived in the past, I lost track of everything important in the present. Being put on academic probation was a wake-up call.

For the first time in my life, I had failed. It didn't matter that I had done so well in high school. The reality was that I had to suck it up, put my ego aside, and accept life for what it was. If I wanted to become something, I had to work hard at it just like everybody else.

This was the first of many failures for me, but the best lesson I learned was that you can start over. No matter how deep of a hole you dig for yourself, you can always start over.

But to do that, you have to keep fighting and trying. No matter how daunting the task may be, you have to put yourself out there. Hall of Fame hockey player Wayne Gretzky once said, ***"You miss 100% of the shots you don't take."***

There are children worldwide who don't have the privilege of a standard education. I had the opportunity to go to college, yet I was acting like a spoiled brat because it wasn't a known institution. If I still believed that I was destined to do something special, then I had to work for it.

Regrets like to manifest themselves as missed opportunities. Every time you make a decision, and it doesn't go your way, it becomes a regret. Success isn't a game of chance; it's a game of numbers. Like famed entrepreneur Mark Cuban once said:

"It doesn't matter how many times you've failed. You just need to be right once."

So then how do you live a life of results and not regrets? For starters, it starts with your mindset. Treat everything in life as an experiment and an experience. There's no pass or fail outcome, just learning. Every experience is an opportunity to learn.

Rejection is tough, and nobody likes it. No matter how many times I've been rejected before, it's a feeling I'll never get used to. I can however, change how it affects me.

In February 2015, I interviewed with Facebook. The entire process spanned three months and was a combination of two phone interviews, a video interview, and an in-person interview. During those three months, I spent every evening after work preparing for each round of interviews.

I even hired an expert to help me prepare for the interview. I was determined to get this job because Facebook was a company I wanted to work for. I felt with Facebook on my resume; it would finally mean that I was talented.

As soon as I finished my last interview, I had a great feeling about it. In my mind I already saw myself as a Facebook employee, everything else was just a formality.

Instead, I didn't get the job. When I asked the recruiter for details, she told me that even though the team liked me, they decided to go with another candidate. I was devastated for weeks.

Then I thought about it. Facebook gets millions of job applications a day. Not only did I get a call-back, but I also went through four rounds of interviews, and made it onsite to interview in person. Instead of being bummed about not getting the job, I should be proud of getting as far as I did.

Sure, I could've sulked around for months, but I didn't. I appreciated what I learned from the experience and moved on with my life. The entire process also taught me how to be better at interviews, and I was grateful for it. This is what I mean by focus on the results.

Life is too short to live with regrets.

#4 Cats Aren't the Only Ones with Nine Lives

There's one fact I know for sure which is one day we will all be dead. Now here's something you didn't know. We all have more than one life; in fact, we have approximately eleven. Let me explain.

It takes roughly about seven years to master something such as a skill, trade, or profession. Now let's say the average person lives to be 88-years-old. After the age of 11, you have eleven opportunities to be great at something.

Check out the table below:

Age	# of years to master something
11-years-old	+7 years
18-years-old	+7 years
25-years-old	+7 years
32-years-old	+7 years
39-years-old	+7 years
46-years-old	+7 years
53-years-old	+7 years
60-years-old	+7 years
67-years-old	+7 years
74-years-old	+7 years
81-years-old	+7 years
88-years-old	Dead

These are your lifelines, and you have eleven of them. You have eleven opportunities to start over at any point in your life. It doesn't matter if you are 18-years-old or 81-years-old. Treat this as a video game. Each lifeline gives you the opportunity to level up and gain new skills and abilities.

Maybe you want to spend one lifeline building a product, spend another lifeline teaching, and then spend one retired on the beach renting scuba gear. That's the amazing thing about your lifelines; you have many opportunities to create a fulfilling life.

I used to have a hard time letting go of the past because I felt like I was missing out on life. I was behind and not where I expected to be. My perspective and how I saw my life, in general, was holding me back.

What makes this new perspective great, is that I can make a mistake, waste one of my lifelines, and still have ten more to start over. You could screw up ten of your lifelines and still have one more to make it all worth it. You have more lives than you think.

Depression, Addiction, and How My 20's Were a Blur

Before we move on, I'd like to share another very personal story with you. When I graduated college in 2004, I was eager to leave my footprint in this world. I also had a girlfriend whom I loved very much and wanted to marry her.

The only problem was that she didn't feel the same way. While she also wanted to change the world she didn't want to do it with me. To her, having a partner meant that she would have to marry and settle down. She wasn't ready for that and ended the relationship shortly after graduation.

She explained that she needed to find herself. She wanted to explore what the world had to offer, and the thought of marriage terrified her. As much as she loved me, this was something she needed to do.

I understood why. I even supported her decision. The last thing I wanted was to marry, have kids, and be unhappy. However, it doesn't change the fact that my heart was still broken in a million pieces.

In college, I took a course on psychology and learned about the five stages of grief. On the surface, it made sense. You start with denial, then anger, move into depression, then bargaining, and finally acceptance. Going through ito however, was a different story.

The worst part is that there's no time limit on how long you stay in each stage. Sometimes it's months and sometimes it's years. At first, I thought she would eventually come back. Maybe she needed a few months to see what life was like without me and come to her senses.

After six months had passed and there wasn't any sign of her coming back, I started to get angry. I wrote her a series of emails, each one angrier than the first. I hated her; I hated that she pulled me into her life and tossed me out as soon as she was done.

I slipped into depression. While in depression, I had a hard time functioning each day. Going to work was such a chore, all I wanted to do was lie in bed and cry myself to sleep. As corny as it sounds, this was how I felt for a very long time.

I needed to find a hobby to distract myself from the pain. Instead of doing something productive like working out, I turned to gambling to numb the pain. Sports betting became the perfect vice for me because I watched sports on TV all the time.

With the added element of gambling, it created the perfect type of distraction I needed. For example, I loved watching professional football but hated watching college football. I didn't know any of the players or the schools.

However, once I made a bet on a team, everything changed because I was invested in a team for three hours. Whether I was watching the game on TV or following the score on the internet, I was completely distracted. The entire experience became an adrenaline rush.

At first, I started with small bets; $50 here and there and I'd win or lose a few hundred each week. It wasn't a big deal when I lost because I rationalized it as paying for entertainment. It was like going to a concert, except I'm in the comfort of my own home.

But then $50 didn't have the same excitement as it did when I first started. I didn't have the same rush anymore. If I won four games, that would only net me $200. Had I doubled or even tripled my bet, I would've won $400 or $600. Like an addict chasing his first high, I started increasing my bets.

I kept increasing my bets every time I felt I wasn't getting the same adrenaline rush. Pretty soon, I was consistently betting $500 per game and sometimes even $1000 or more.

The thing about gambling, in general, is that it's set up so that the odds are against you. Whether you are playing slots or blackjack, the house always has a small advantage over you.

The same goes for sports betting. The odds you use for betting always favors the bookies. I thought I could beat the bookie because I researched, followed trends, and looked for angles. However, it all ended with me losing tons of money.

I would win $1000 one week and lose $3000 the following week. At the peak of my addiction I would win $5000 on Tuesday and by Friday lose all of that plus another $5000 of my own money. What started off as a distraction from my breakup turned into a full-blown addiction.

None of my friends and family knew how bad it was. On the surface I was a guy with a well-paying job and a normal life, but behind the curtains was a different story. I would spend my nights and weekends betting on anything I could find.

On Saturdays, during college football season, I would stay in my apartment all day watching and betting on sports. My day started at 8am and would run all the way until midnight. Because I was so addicted, I would bet on European soccer games at 4am because it was the only sport that was happening at that time.

Gambling also took a toll on me physically. I was pretty fit in my 20's; working out several times a week. Once I got hooked on sports betting, I stopped going to the gym. My diet went down the drain. All I ate was fast food and unhealthy snacks. I gained a lot of weight from this.

In the span of eight years, I estimate I probably lost over $250k. I depleted all my savings, racked up tons of credit card bills, and borrowed from my friends and family to pay my gambling debts. It took such a mental and emotional toll on me. Not only was I still reeling from the breakup, but I was also stressed out because I had no money and in debt.

I constantly beat myself up for being so stupid.

My 20's were supposed to be the prime years of my life, and instead I wasted it away addicted to gambling. I was trapped in my own prison and trying to see the light at the end of the tunnel was impossible. It wasn't until I met my wife that I was able to finally get help.

When I met my wife, she gave me a reason to be better and fight for the life I deserve. Because of her, I got professional help, did six months of addiction therapy, and got my life back together.

I'm happy to say that as of today, I don't have the slightest urge to gamble and I'm completely debt free. I'm finally learning to sit back and enjoy life for once.

#5 Stop Victimizing Yourself, Stop Blaming Others

I touched on this a bit earlier in my first story, but let's spend more time diving into this topic. It's important because people who can't let go of the past often victimize themselves and blame others for their failures. I know because I was one of them.

For example, I would constantly blame my dad if things didn't go well for me. I would victimize myself because I didn't want to accept the truth. Sure, what he said hurt my feelings, but at the end of the day, I'm responsible for my actions.

I wanted a scapegoat, a reason other than myself to explain why things didn't go my way. It's easier to convince yourself that someone else is at fault instead of accepting blame. You see this a lot in children when they get in trouble and are afraid to deal with the consequences.

When I became addicted to gambling, I refused to take accountability for my actions. I blamed my ex-girlfriend for breaking my heart and turning me towards sports betting. I blamed my parents for not knowing what was going on. Even if I knew none of this was true, it made me feel better about my life.

When I met my wife, we got into arguments about my gambling. I would blame her for not being sensitive. I made her feel that she needed to handle me a certain way otherwise I would blow up like a ticking time bomb. Eventually, she got tired of it and threatened to leave if I didn't get help.

Victimizing yourself only goes so far. Maybe at first you get your way because people feel guilty for you, but the act starts to wear thin. You think you can make mistakes and blame others for your problems, but eventually, people will leave. If you don't start growing up and taking accountability for your actions, you'll never be able to move forward.

#6 Make the Most of the Time You Have Now

I once asked in an online forum, *"How do I make up for lost time?"* Because of my gambling addiction, my 20's were spent doing nothing productive with my life. Of all the replies I received, this was the best response I got:

"You can't make up for lost time; you can only make the most of the time you have now."

All those years I spent dealing with my addiction and depression, I know I'll never get back. As a result, I constantly wonder how my life would've been had I never got caught up with betting.

Perhaps I would be much farther in my career.

I know there's no way you can make up for lost time, but when I asked the question, I was looking for someone to console me. I wanted someone to give me hope, snap me out of my negative thinking, and force me to start living in the present. Fortunately, someone did slap some sense into me.

Part of the science behind moving on is learning to let go. I kept replaying in my mind over, and over again, a life I could've lived if not for gambling. But living with regret only held me back from moving on. What I needed to do was look at the time I had left and start figuring out how to make the most of it.

By creating new experiences, you replace the unpleasant memories you hold onto, with better ones.

We all live once so we should live this life to the fullest. This doesn't mean doing something stupid that will jeopardize the well-being of your life. It means living a life where you can look back and be proud of what you've accomplished. It means living a life where you have no regrets.

I find it strange that some people are afraid to live until they are faced with their own mortality. We shouldn't have to wait until we're dying or about to die to do all the things we want to do in life. We should begin doing it today.

A friend of mine passed away from cancer at the young age of 26. One day he was rushed to the hospital with severe stomach pains and found out he had stage three, stomach cancer. Can you imagine the shock he was in coming into the hospital only to find out he was dying?

He went from having his whole life in front of him to figuring out what he wanted to do with the limited time he had left. He did not give up hope, but at the same time, he knew what the reality of the situation was. He knew what he was up against; we all did.

He fought as hard as he could and even towards the end he never gave up. Unfortunately, he couldn't beat cancer and several months later he passed away. He never got to live his life to the fullest, and I use it as a reminder to make each day count.

There are going to be things that frustrated you. There are going to be things that upset you. But you have the power to decide how long you let them affect you. Don't sweat the small stuff. Your time is precious; it's the only thing in this world you can't have back.

Embrace Your Mistakes

"Once we embrace our limits, we go beyond them" – Albert Einstein

When Life Gives You Lemons, Grab Some Salt and Tequila

Do you remember the old saying, *"When life gives you lemons, you make lemonade?"* Well, what if life gave you lemons and you didn't even know it? What if you went about with your life as if it were normal only to find out years later that it wasn't?

How would that change your outlook?

Do you start freaking out because everything you've known to be true isn't? Or do you brush it off since your life has been totally fine even before finding out you it wasn't normal?

Besides, who's to tell you what normal is nowadays?

Growing up I had these strange habits. I can't really explain what they are. When I feel an urge to do these habits, I have to do them. These habits also tend to change over time.

Whether it's repeating a word over and over again or flicking my pinky quickly, these are some of my habits. I can't explain why I do these things; I just have to do them. If I don't, an overwhelming feeling of stress and anxiety comes over me.

It feels like not being able to breathe. Doing these habits are a necessity because I can't control them. Sometimes they take a toll on me physically. For example, if I'm always making a motion with my wrist, it gets tired, and I feel like I have carpal tunnel syndrome.

It also takes a toll on me mentally and emotionally as well. Some people look at me funny when they see me constantly blinking or wriggling my nose. Because of this, I try hard not to do these habits when speaking face-to-face.

The toughest part is knowing that I'm the only person in my immediate family, my extended family, and my group of friends that has this problem. Even growing up, I never met another person with the same condition. I accepted this because I had no choice; this was how I was born.

For most of my life, I learned to live with these habits and work around it. As I got older, I no longer had to repeat words, but I still had the physical habits. To deal with this, I would try to keep a straight face for as long as possible when talking to people. Then I would turn away as if I'm coughing if I needed to squint my eyes or do something unnatural with my face.

I knew I was different, but because I couldn't explain how or why. I never made a big deal about it. I figured if it were something major, my parents would've taken me to see a doctor as a child. Since it hadn't bothered me for years, I was content with living with my condition as an adult.

That is until I saw a TV show in 2002 that would reveal something I didn't know about myself. The show was called 'MTV True Life' where they profiled the real lives of people who share a common predicament. For example, some of the episodes and topics would be:

- *True Life: I'm a Homeless Teenager*
- *True Life: I'm Addicted to Videogames*
- *True Life: My Parents Are Divorced*
- *True Life: I'm in Love with my Best Friend*

What I like most about this show was that it was authentic. It captured real people in their daily lives dealing with real problems. I watched this show all the time, but this night would be different.

The title was called *True Life: I Have Tourette's.*

I was 22-years-old at the time. All I knew about Tourette's growing up was how Hollywood portrayed this condition. In the movies, people with Tourette's were depicted as swearing uncontrollably. In fact, I had never met anyone with Tourette's until I got to college and he fit the bill of what a person with Tourette's was like.

At least, that was until I watched this episode of MTV True Life.
When we think of Tourette's syndrome and how it's portrayed on TV, those are extreme cases. There are different types of Tourette's, which range from mild to severe. Also, the way Tourette's affects a person can vary. Some people have motor tics, some have vocal tics, and others have both.

A tic is defined as: *"a sudden, repetitive, non-rhythmic motor movement or vocalization involving discrete muscle groups."* You can think of this as a twitch, a facial grimace, blinking, clearing your throat, or grunting. Someone with Tourette's will have both motor and vocal tics.

When I was watching this episode of True Life, I was expecting to see people who cursed nonstop. While there was one gentleman who did, the other people on the show didn't fit the bill; in fact, only a small percentage of people with Tourette's cuss uncontrollably.

But it wasn't the vocal tics that stood out to me; it was the motor tics. These people had a hard time functioning on a daily basis, because they had uncontrollable movement of their bodies and faces. Imagine trying to write a letter but you can't because you're always shaking your wrist. You don't want to do it because it makes your hand tired, but you can't stop.

That's how Tourette's affected me.

As I watched this episode, it was almost like watching my entire life story unfold. Growing up, I knew there was always something different with me, but I couldn't figure out what. I never thought much of it and lived my life the best way I knew how.

But now I knew what was wrong with me, and it made me cry.

I cried because I was relieved. For the first time in over twenty years, I finally knew why I was different. There was a name for my condition. I also cried because I was angry at the world. Why me? Why was I cursed with a condition that was incurable? What did I do to deserve this?

Life gave me lemons, but I wasn't going to let it keep me down.

#7 Stop Making Problems Bigger Than They Are

After the shock of finding out I had Tourette's, I immediately started researching on the internet to educate myself on my condition. I went through as many websites as I could to find and even joined a few forums to talk to other people with Tourette's. I needed to know if it was something that could be cured.

We have all these advancements in science and medicine; surely there had to be a way to cure Tourette's. Instead, everything I found was very discouraging. Tourette's is a neurological disorder and therefore is incurable. I was stuck with this condition for life.

"Okay," I thought, *"but there has to be a way to treat it."*

I made an appointment to see my doctor as quickly as possible. During the visit, I felt like she didn't care that I had this condition. She didn't bother referring me to a neurologist or someone who had more knowledge in this field. I was for answers and instead, I was given a prescription and sent home.

I didn't even bother picking up my meds. Everything I read about Tourette's already told me what I needed to know. I learned that people who took the meds quickly stopped because of the severe side effects. I didn't want to be a zombie. I didn't want any of this; there had to be another way.

I went home and continued searching the internet until I found this particular forum for people with Tourette's, and parents of children with Tourette's. They were sharing knowledge and tips on how to treat the condition with supplements and vitamins instead of meds. There was a lady named Bonnie Grimaldi who discovered a combination of vitamins and supplements that worked for her son.

These supplements couldn't stop the tics but helped to keep the tics to a minimum. I thought this was perfect. If I could reduce my tics by even 50 percent, I'll take it. She had a website where she sold these supplements and I immediately became a customer.

The supplements weren't cheap, but I didn't care. I was desperate for a solution. For three months, I took the supplements daily. During those three months, nothing changed. Even if I felt a small improvement, I would have kept going, but I didn't feel anything. My tics were still present and as active as ever.

I began to get depressed because of this. From reading the forums, it seemed like the supplements were working for some people yet it didn't work for me. I remembered sitting in my room, frustrated at the fact that I would be this freak for the rest of my life. It wasn't fair. What did I do to deserve this?

For the next few months, I was very withdrawn. I avoided talking face to face with people because I was always wondering what they thought of me. Did they notice my facial tics? Are they talking negatively about me behind my back? My Tourette's made me very insecure about myself.

Then one day I got tired of feeling sorry for myself. I needed a reality check to put things into perspective. My life was fine before I watched that episode of MTV True Life. Sure I was different, but I was a happy guy who was different. My family and friends never thought any less of me.

Why did everything change once I was able to put a label on my condition? I was still the same person. Was it all in my head?

Then that's when it hit me; I was making my problems out to be bigger than they were. Growing up nobody had a problem with my Tourette's. Sure I was made fun of as a kid, but what kid hasn't been made fun of. I had lived with this condition for most of my life. So, why all of a sudden, did it bother me now?

Because I let it bother me.

I let this condition bother me when it had been an afterthought for most of my life. I needed to find a silver lining in all of this chaos. My Tourette's was moderate. It could've been worse. I could have vocal tics that make it impossible for me to hold a conversation with anyone. I could be cursing uncontrollably.

Instead, I happen to squint and wriggle my nose every few seconds. It wasn't all that bad. So I decided to accept my condition; the secret lemons life had given me. Rather than try to find a cure or treatment, I educated myself more on Tourette's to have a better understanding of how to live with it.

I learned to avoid caffeine because caffeine tends to make my tics more active. I learned to deal with stress better because stress makes my tics more active. I learned how to accept who I've always been and to stop making my problems bigger than they actually are.

Yes, I have Tourette's, but Tourette's doesn't have me.

The biggest lesson I learned was that if it didn't bother other people before, then there was no reason for it to bother me now, in the future, or ever again.

#8 Be True to Yourself and Own Who You Are

Before I knew I had Tourette's, I never thought much of my condition. Now that I could put a name to it, I felt like I was hiding a secret. My biggest concern was passing it onto my kids. I can live with Tourette's since it doesn't cause any major discomfort to my daily life, but what about my future kids?

What if they inherit Tourette's and it becomes extreme for them? When I found out I had Tourette's, I also had a girlfriend. When I finally opened up and shared with her what I discovered, she looked at me and said,

"It's okay. I always knew there was something different about you but it doesn't bother me."

Here I was agonizing for months over my condition, trying to find a cure, and the only person who was bothered by all this was me. My girlfriend didn't see me any differently and, to an extent, she thought it was cute. In her eyes, my condition made me special.

In fact, every girlfriend who I've shared this secret with, has never had a problem with it. My wife makes me laugh when it comes to my condition because she teases me about it in a very loving way. She understands the possibility that our kids might inherit Tourette's, but doesn't let it bother her. She loves me for who I am.

My biggest take-away from living with this condition is that it's all in my head. Before I knew what it was called, I had a regular life. Outside of my tics everything else was normal. It wasn't until I watched that episode of MTV True

Life did I begin to panic and feel like something serious was wrong with me.

Once I accepted who I was and how to live with Tourette's, my life went back to normal. Now I feel more confident enough to say, *"yes I have Tourette's and yes I have a great life."* One of my goals as an entrepreneur is to help others who have Tourette's or similar mental conditions get over their insecurities and achieve their goals as well.

Be true to yourself. Own who you are and don't be embarrassed of the person looking back at you in the mirror. When you are confident, other people will sense that. If you are insecure or have low self-esteem, they will sense that too.

When you own who you are, despite of your flaws and shortcomings, people will respect you even more. That's because they see how confident and comfortable you are in your own skin. It makes them comfortable with their own insecurities.

These days when people look at me funny or if I think they have a question about my tics, I just tell them I have Tourette's. That usually does the job and it's a relief knowing I don't have to wonder what people are thinking anymore. People are generally afraid of what they don't know and in my case, I try my best to educate them.

Trust me, confidence is infectious. People say humor is infectious but I think confidence is just as contagious. When you own who you are, that confidence is projected to those around you. As a result, you will be a highly confident person.

At the end of the day, it's about being honest and true to yourself.

#9 Use Your Story to Inspire Others

For the longest time, I was extremely embarrassed by my gambling addiction and the financial ruin it caused. I was in my early thirties with no savings, tons of debt, and a career that wasn't going anywhere. Every time I tried to take a step forward, my gambling addiction caused me to take five steps backward.

It also didn't help that the majority of my friends were also addicted to gambling too. Even the times I tried to quit, it was hard because being around them and watching sports caused me to get pulled back into gambling.

It wasn't until I met my wife, did I finally seek help. By making the decision, to go to therapy, I admitted that I had a problem and needed help. I wasn't afraid or embarrassed by this fact. I was just tired of struggling. I made it known to my friends that I was going to therapy and wouldn't come around as much anymore.

Some understood, and some didn't. Some supported me, and some didn't care. However, I had one friend who reached out and asked me how therapy was going. When he saw the progress I was making, he asked for the contact info to my therapist so that he could go as well. This made me ecstatic.

I was proud that I inspired my friend to get this life in order, even though I was far from getting my life together. Just the fact that I took the initiative to get help was enough motivation for him to get started too. I was his motivation even though I didn't do much.

Everybody has a story to tell that is capable of inspiring others; even if you don't think it's worthy of it. There are many people out there with lofty goals and aspirations. Who wouldn't love to be a visionary like Steve Jobs or Elon Musk? The challenge is figuring out how to become like the people you admire?

It's like waking up and deciding you want to climb Mount Everest when you've never hiked your entire life. What most people need is to figure out how to get to that next level. I'm sure my friend also thought about quitting gambling many times, but it wasn't until he saw me taking initiative did he do something about it.

To him, I was that next level. I wasn't someone who was preaching how to quit gambling. I was a guy who took steps to start quitting. I laid out the path for him to follow with my actions. I was able to inspire him to get help by helping myself. This is what I mean by using your story to inspire others.

One of my reasons for writing this book is to help and inspire others like you with my story. I don't have it all figured out yet. I'm not a millionaire hot shot or anything close. I'm just a guy who made his share of mistakes but finally turning his life around.

If I could help just one person turn their life around, then all the effort it took to write this book would be worth it. Now it's your turn; think about all that you've overcome in your life. No matter how big or small the challenge, what is your story?

What can you do to help and inspire others?

#10 Happiness on the Inside Equals Happiness on the Outside

Do you ever wonder why miserable people stay miserable and happy people never sweat the small stuff? That's because how you feel on the inside has a direct effect on how you feel on the outside. If you're unhappy on the inside, it will show in how you interact with the people around you.

In the beginning of our relationship, my wife and I fought a lot. I would say that the majority of it, was because of me. We fought because of my gambling addiction, but we also fought because I hated myself; because I couldn't accept responsibility, I projected that hatred towards her instead.

I always victimized myself during our fights and the only way I knew how to win was to scream louder than her. I blamed her for how I felt. She backed down many times because she didn't want me to get angrier than I was.

Even though I may have won the argument, I was losing the war. All the fighting made her lose respect for me and created a rift between us. She described being with me, 'was like walking on eggshells all the time.' She never knew what would set me off and how I would react.

She would say something that generally wouldn't bothered me, but if I was having a bad day, I took it out on her. I was so unpredictable; like a ticking time bomb. I hated that she felt this way, but what I hated more was that I couldn't do anything to fix it.

My unhappiness bled into other areas of my life and made it difficult for me to maintain relationships with those closest to me. I directed my anger and grief at others even when they had nothing to do with it. I was a wreck.

If you're miserable on the inside, you're going to look miserable on the outside. If you're angry on the inside, you're going to get mad at others on the outside. Your loved ones will love you and support you for who you are, but everyone has their limits.

Pretty soon, you're going to find yourself alone because that's what almost happened to me. There was a particular fight where I had a feeling that my wife was at her limit. Rather than cry because she was hurt, she simply didn't care anymore. I was very close to losing her.

Since beating my addiction and getting out of debt, my life has completely changed. I no longer feel any guilt or shame. Instead, it's replaced with a sense of relief and calmness. Little things, no longer irritate me, and my relationship with my wife has been the best it's ever been. This is all due to how I feel about myself now.

Being happy begins with giving yourself the opportunity and permission to do so. During the darkest periods of my life, I wouldn't allow myself to be happy. I kept punishing myself mentally and emotionally because I felt like I deserved what was happening to me.

I made myself believe that being unhappy and miserable was the only option I had. I made myself believe that I had to suffer for my mistakes. This was farther from the truth. We all have a right to be happy regardless of how many times we fall in life.

It starts with how you feel about yourself and what you allow yourself to feel. Be happy with who you are even if it may not seem like much in the beginning. Keep that positive thinking until you start seeing changes in your life. Pretty soon, you will become that happy person and won't need to tell yourself to be happy.

It will all happen naturally.

Making Your Comeback

"No matter how far you travel in the wrong direction, you can always turn around." – Unknown

When You're Going Through Hell, Keep Going

At the peak of my addiction and depression, I struggled with thoughts of suicide. Not just once or twice, but daily. I had these thoughts several times a day, for months on end. I felt so worthless that if a car crashed into me and took my life, I wouldn't mind.

I thought about different ways of dying; quick ones like jumping off the roof of a tall building and painless ones like ingesting a whole bottle of Tylenol. I was in so much emotional pain that dying seemed like a better alternative than living a sad and depressing life.

When you can't think clearly and hate your life, any option, even death, sounds like a better alternative to living. That's how scary it was for me; I couldn't stop the negative thoughts.

I was a disappointment to my family. I should've been further in my career but wasn't. I couldn't imagine anyone wanting to marry me since I was such a loser. I didn't want to give up, but I was tired of fighting. I had been struggling with gambling for eight years and kept moving backward every time I tried to quit.

I felt like my life was never going to change. I was forever destined to be in debt and gamble myself into an early grave. What made it tough was that I was too proud to get help. I always felt like I could beat the addiction alone. I was also in denial that I had a problem. Therapy? Forget about it.

I racked up so much credit card debt from gambling that my credit score was ruined. Some friends avoided me because they knew eventually I would make up a sob story and ask to borrow money. I even lied to my employer to get pay advances to pay my gambling debts.

Nobody had a clue about how bad my situation was; not my family, nor my friends. Some people knew but not to what extent. Nobody knew about my suicidal thoughts. My cousin thought about staging an intervention for me, but decided against it because he was afraid of how I would react.

In hindsight, he should've still done it, but I would've probably be too stubborn to listen. For some people, like myself, we only learn the hard way. Change must come from within. I'm only here today because I hit rock bottom and finally got professional help.

My life was hell for eight years and somehow I managed to make it out okay. I survived, and if I can do it, you can too. When I had nothing, the only thing I could hold onto was hope. Hope for a better tomorrow, hope for a second chance at life.

You have to keep fighting even when you feel like there's nothing left to fight for. You have to keep pushing even when you feel like you're pushing against a concrete wall. As long as you have oxygen in your veins, you have a fighting chance at turning it all around.

#11 Start Small, Start Now

There were many days when I woke up and wondered, *"what the heck happened to me?"* No, I'm not referring to being hung over from too much drinking. I'm talking about waking up and wondering how my life became such a disaster.

I tried to quit gambling on my own many times, but every time I thought about how much debt I was in, I got discouraged. I needed to find a way to pay off $60,000 worth of debt fast. Because I couldn't make more money or save enough, I relapsed back into gambling. As stupid as it sounds, I thought I could win $60,000 to pay off my debts.

Here's the thing about gambling, you'll always lose no matter what. It didn't matter that I won $5,000 in a week because I would lose $10,000 the following week. Looking back, I was such an idiot. I gambled to try to get out of debt, only to cause myself to fall into more debt.

How stupid is that?

It's easy to point the finger now and talk about how foolish I was, but during that time I couldn't see an easy way out of debt. Going to therapy helped me quit gambling but the debt I racked up over the years was still there. Whenever I thought about my debt, I would try to think of ways to make a quick buck.

This method never worked. In fact, I got into deeper debt because of it. I had to be realistic about my situation. I didn't accumulate $60,000 worth of debt overnight; it took time to get there.

Using the same line of thinking, it would take time for me to get out of debt.

There were two options to pay off this debt.

1. Reduce my spending, budget, and save money each month to pay off my debt.

2. Try to increase my monthly income to pay off this debt faster.

I was already budgeting and saving money each month to pay off my debt, but it wasn't making a dent. Gambling to pay off my debt was a terrible idea and created more debt. My only other option was to increase my monthly income, but how? I couldn't go to my boss and ask for a raise.

One way was to get another job, but how would I make it work? I was already working 40 hours a week. Even if I found another job, I don't think I could physically make it work? There just weren't enough hours in the day.

I had read books about people who consult for a living. They make tons of money and only work several hours a week. This sounded like a pretty good alternative but what would I consult on? Famed entrepreneur and investor Mark Cuban once told a story about how he was consulting for companies on how to set up their computer equipment.

He realized early on, that many of his clients could've solved their own problems, had they opted to read the manual. Instead, he made tons of money solving their problems by simply reading the manual and following the directions. I decided to take the same approach.

During this time, I had been reading and learning about SEO, which stands for Search Engine Optimization. It is the science behind how websites are ranked on Google search result pages. Imagine you have a website that sells TV's, and you're ranked on Google as the very first website under flat screen televisions.

How many visits would you get as the first result? How much money would you make off of those visits? This is why SEO is critical to online businesses. The problem, though, was that I didn't have an online business to apply what I learned. Instead, I had to look for other people with online businesses who could use my help.

My first client was my dentist. It was great because I didn't have to try and sell him my services. I just built on the existing relationship we already had. I convinced him to let me help increase his website traffic and get more patients. I'm not an SEO expert, but whatever I learned, I applied it to his site. I was learning by doing.

The good news was that he didn't mind that I wasn't an expert. Because he trusted me, he was okay letting me try various tactics. Some of them worked, and some didn't. As long as I was getting him results, everything was fine. And that's exactly what I did.

Soon after, he referred me to other people he knew and slowly I grew my consulting business. After about three months, I was making an extra three thousand each month. Had I waited until I was an expert in SEO, I never would've had this opportunity to build a side business.

By keeping my day job, scaling down my lifestyle, and doing consulting on the side, I paid off all of my debts in just fourteen months. It was an amazing feeling. The day I became debt free was the day I officially started over again. I now had a clean slate to rebuild my life.

You'll never be ready so you might as well start now and start small. Treat everything as an experiment and whether you succeed or not at first, it's all about learning and building momentum.

#12 Change Your Environment to Change Your Life

Turning your life around isn't solely about the changes you need to make to yourself. It also requires changes to your environment. They say that you are the average of the five people you hang out with the most. Take a minute and think about the five people you spend the most time with.

Is this accurate? Are you the average of the five people you hang out with the most?

One of the first things I learned in therapy was to remove any triggers from my environment that might cause me to relapse. Because my friends were also into sports betting and sports in general, this meant that I had to stay away from them whenever sports were involved.

This was extremely tough for me because it meant avoiding most of my friends. It was also tough because we hung out a lot. For example, on Sundays, we would put some meat on the grill, grab a few beers, and watch football. It was our ritual for over fifteen years; we did this before we got involved with gambling.

But my therapist advised that I avoid them altogether, especially since they also gambled. There was no compromise or middle ground. I wasn't trying to control my gambling; I wanted to stop completely. If I was serious about getting past my gambling addiction, I had to make this sacrifice.

When I told my friends about therapy and how I couldn't come around anymore, some understood and some didn't. The ones who didn't felt that I could still come and hang out. They reasoned that I didn't need to bet, but I told them it wasn't the point. I couldn't be around that type of environment. I didn't want to get influenced into betting again.

The first month was tough. It was like mourning a death of a loved one. I went from having friends to no longer having friends. Suddenly, there was this huge void in my life. I didn't know how long I had to avoid my friends, but if I wanted to get better, this needed to be done.

I hated this feeling. I hated the fact that I was trying to turn my life around and losing friends was a result. You hear stories about people going through painful physical withdrawals from drugs. I felt like I was going through a mental and emotional withdrawal from my friends.

There were a few times when I broke down to my wife telling her this wasn't fair, but that's the price I had to pay if I was serious about getting over my addiction. About six months into my treatment, I decided I needed to focus my attention elsewhere. Being depressed wasn't helping the situation.

I always had an entrepreneurial spirit. I would spend hours reading about entrepreneurs like Steve Jobs and Mark Zuckerberg and get inspired. However, I was afraid to start something by myself. I always felt more confident working with others.

Because my friends weren't entrepreneurial, I had nobody to talk to or bounce ideas off of. It was also hard for me to express this part of myself so I ended up suppressing it. For the longest time, I was a dreamer who never took any action.

Then something in me changed because of therapy. Since my friends weren't a big part of my life anymore, I had to fill that void somehow. That loneliness became so unbearable that it forced me to get over my fear of being alone and find others who were also entrepreneurial.

I call this finding your tribe. Find people who you want to be like, those who share the same goals and aspirations as you do. They are the people who are going to help you get there by being in your life and inspiring you to take action. They are the ones who are going to push you when you need it the most because they understand. They identify with who you are.

I love my friends, but I also know that there are some parts of me that they won't completely understand, like my entrepreneurial spirit. Rather than dwell on my loneliness, I devoted my attention and energy on finding my tribe and bringing the entrepreneur inside of me out.

I attended my very first hackathon workshop where my team won and the product we built raised close to a million dollars in funding. From there I signed up to be a local organizer in San Francisco where I organized and hosted workshops teaching entrepreneurs how to build products people want.

Being an organizer helped me build my network because I had access to more entrepreneurs. I value quality over quantity because it's about finding the right people, not just more people. Those same entrepreneurs ended up being friends and mentors to me. That's how I found my tribe of movers and shakers that supported me in my entrepreneurial endeavors.

In a span of over two years, I went from being a guy who was lost in his career to a guy who gained confidence in his abilities with each passing day. I finally found my passion and that was being an entrepreneur creating value for other people.

When I first started, it was about being better and getting over my addiction. Then I quickly saw how critical my environment was to both my current and future goals. In addition to beating my addiction, I found my true calling as an entrepreneur.

None of this would have been possible had I not made the initial change to my environment.

#13 How a Four-Letter Word Can Spark Change

It took eight years and losing over $250,000 before I got professional help. When I think back, it's hard to understand why I took as long as I did. I know however, a big part of it, had to do with my ego. Because I was used to being an overachiever growing up, it was very hard for me to admit defeat. I especially didn't want to admit to a gambling addiction.

I can accept Tourette's because it's who I am and something I was born with. I didn't want to be a degenerate gambler, but it's who I became due to poor life choices. That was hard to swallow even though I knew deep down it was the truth.

I soon learned that a four-letter-word could ignite change in my life. That word is "help."

Not enough people ask for help when they should. Even the most successful individuals in this world couldn't get to where they are today without help. My help came in the form of my wife, my therapist, and my tribe. They are the ones who pushed me when I needed it most.

We live in a society where asking for help is considered a weakness. I'm here to tell you it's the complete opposite. Understanding when you are at your limit, is being strong. Admitting that you need help to keep youself going, is being strong. Realizing that you can achieve more with others. is being strong.

Let's say you're ready to turn your life around and you need the help of others, where do you start? It depends on what aspect of your life you are looking to change. Are you dealing with some sort of addiction or trauma? If so, get professional help right away.

Are you trying to ignite your career or find your passion? Seek like-minded people and find your tribe. There are tons of resources on the Internet such as Facebook groups, LinkedIn groups, and Meetup groups where you can meet like-minded people.

Maybe you're looking for clarity because your life is foggy at the moment. Find someone whom you trust to be your support buddy and open up to him or her. Have that person be your accountability partner. It works even better when you can be accountability partners for each other.

At the end of the day, it's about opening up and allowing others into your life. Alone we can only do so much, but together we can achieve much more. If you're not ready to ask for help then offer to help someone. You'll be surprised at how helping someone get his or her life together will spark you to get your life together.

#14 Keep One Eye on the Past and One on the Future

The past can be a tricky thing to deal with. Some people have traumatic experiences that they choose to forget the past. Others lock it away in the corner of their minds refusing to admit it ever happened. Others become so scarred that they hold onto the past and refuse to move on.

For me, I regularly held onto the past as a daily reminder why I deserved to be miserable. I knew it wasn't healthy for me, but I couldn't help it. I was punishing myself for all the mistakes I made. I could never see a bright future for myself.

Every time I looked in the mirror, I saw a huge disappointment. I saw a failure; someone who had so much potential but squandered it away. People say you should be proud of the things you have in life, but I had nothing. My life was empty.

For eight years, I beat myself up every day. I convinced myself that I didn't deserve better. It wasn't until I went to therapy, did I give myself a chance to look towards the future.

Now that I'm able to look back at the past, I'm proud of what happened. Beating a gambling addiction, being debt free, and pushing myself to follow my dreams happened because I chose to get help.

The struggle made me resilient and taught me more about myself that I ever knew. The struggle showed me that I could overcome anything as long as I kept fighting. It's because of the struggle I'll never forget the lessons I learned.

As you're working on turning your life around, take note of how you're slowly changing. Focus on the little things that you're doing right. Sure you may get 7 out of 10 things wrong but those three things that you did well, celebrate them. Use them as a springboard going forward.

The past is meant to help us prepare for the future. Even some of the greatest tragedies in history are memorialized to remind us of what not to do or what not to repeat. Don't run away from your past, embrace it because it's a part of you. Learn from it.

When you keep one eye on the past, you're using it as a reminder of how much you've overcome. Sometimes it can be painful to look at the past, but the pain is there to make us stronger. Use it to keep one eye on the future and continue moving forward with the lessons you have learned.

#15 Invest in Yourself for the Greatest Return Possible

Living in Silicon Valley, I'm always reading stories about people in their 20's who are building million dollar companies. Sometimes it makes me sad knowing that most of my 20's was spent gambling and struggling to make sense out of my life.

Now that I'm much older, I have a hard time not comparing myself to these younger prodigies. It's just my competitive nature. I know dwelling on the past doesn't help me move ahead, so to stay competitive I need to invest in myself.

From my experience, college doesn't prepare you for life; at least not the type of life that I want to live. College prepares you to work. Once you start working, you're still not prepared for life. All those years I spent working, the only thing I learned was how to work. If you took me out of the workplace, I didn't have much to offer.

There's so much more to life than work. What about doing meaningful work? What about creating and adding value to others? What about building a legacy that you can be proud to share with your children? College doesn't help you with any of that.

What happens if I want to start my own company and leave my footprint in this world? What happens if I want to chase freedom and passion instead of money and recognition? Where do I go to learn these valuable life lessons?

They don't teach this in school, and they certainly don't explain this in the workplace. This is why it is important to invest in yourself. What exactly does it mean to invest in yourself? Congratulations you're already doing so by reading this book

Here are more examples of investing in yourself:

- **Education:** Going to college was something I did because it was expected of me. However, once I graduated, I regret not taking the time to further my education. This doesn't mean that you have to go back to school. There are tons of resources on the Internet, and classes you can take online. The more skills you develop and master, the more valuable you are.

- **Reading:** The only time I ever read was in school because I had to. I didn't start reading for pleasure until just a few years ago. I wish I had started sooner because reading is a great form of education. We should always be learning. The more knowledge you can instill in yourself, the better off you'll be.

- **Fitness:** When I was younger, I worked out a lot. However, once I got caught up in gambling, I stopped. Now that I'm older, I realize the importance of fitness. Try to squeeze in at least 30 minutes of exercise each day, whether its weight training or going for a quick jog. You'll be surprised at how much sharper you feel once you start a fitness regimen.

- **Eating Right:** Dieting and fitness go hand in hand. In addition to not working out, I also started eating poorly. As a result, I gained a lot of weight. I'm working on eating healthier now, but you should start eating healthy as soon as you can. Remember the saying, "garbage in garbage out"? Put some real brain food into your body.

- **Get Plenty of Sleep:** I hated sleeping as a child but now that I'm older, I value a good night's sleep. When I was depressed, I rarely got good sleep. I was always worried about my future. Eventually, the lack of sleep led me to more poor decision making. These days when I feel myself getting tired, I choose to sleep earlier so I can wake up the next day feeling refreshed.

These are just a few examples of how to invest in yourself. The point I'm making is that you have to start taking care of yourself today if you want to turn your life around. You are your biggest competitive advantage, so keep that mind sharp, that body strong, and kicking butt.

#16 Creating a Blueprint for Success

Turning your life around doesn't happen overnight. When you're focused and determined, it doesn't take that long either. From the time I sought help, until today, it's been a little over two years. In that short amount of time, I've done more than I ever could have imagined.

Here are the tips that have worked in setting myself up for future success.

First, understand that the core of all change is action. Simply wanting change or thinking about it won't work. You need to push yourself to take action and continue to take action. Doing something once or twice isn't good enough. Build momentum, take that action and snowball it into sustained change.

Create healthy habits so that they become a part of your daily routine. During the four months where I sought help for my gambling addiction, I learned a lot about how addictions work in general. Whether the addiction is physical or mental, everything starts in the brain.

Think about your favorite junk food. When you eat your favorite junk food, the first thing you notice is how it tastes in your mouth. For me, I like to snack on pork rinds, and eating it starts with the crunch of texture followed by a salty and spicy taste.

These are the taste buds on your tongue sending signals up to your brain. Once you get this euphoric sensation, your brain releases a chemical called dopamine. Dopamine is a hormone that helps control the brain's reward and pleasure centers. When you snack on your favorite junk food, your brain is rewarding your body by making you feel good.

Have you ever wondered about how kids can't seem to get enough sugar? This is similar to how addiction works. Your brain releases a feeling of euphoria when you are performing the addicted behavior. In my case, the thought of gambling got my heart racing.

Just thinking about betting on a game made me both excited and anxious at the same time. This sensation was heightened because money was on the line. The more money I had at stake, the more excited I became. Because I kept repeating this activity over time, my brain automatically linked gambling to the feeling of excitement. This is how addiction is created.

Now, to set yourself up for future success, take the same concept but replace the harmful activity with a healthy one. Begin associating the euphoric feeling with healthy habits. Ever wonder how some people get a runner's high or a natural high from exercise? Again, it's our brain releasing dopamine because it associates working out with feeling good.

When you create a blueprint for success, look for small wins that you can be proud of. Associate the feelings of excitement and happiness to the small wins. Make it so that you continue working towards small wins. Who doesn't like to win and feel good?

These days whenever I have a rough day or feel stuck in a rut, I stop what I'm doing and take a minute to reflect. I look back at how much I've accomplished and what I've been able to overcome. Those are my small wins and they help me reset and get focused.

Small wins lead to big successes, so don't underestimate the power of little accomplishments. You're working on creating the foundation for sustained future success.

#17 How to Begin Today

Up until now, I've shared a few personal stories on what I did to turn my life around. I've also given you several tips and strategies on what to do. The next step is for you to begin putting it all together.

My recommendation is to take one or two tips and start working on it until it becomes routine. Don't try to do too much at once. I want you to focus on the quality of the tips you try and not how many of them you are doing.

What you want to look for is a good flow. A good flow is when you get into a rhythm, all the while making improvements to your lifestyle. Even the smallest increase in your lifestyle is a win.

For example, here's what you could start out with to get into a good flow. Add at least 30 minutes of exercise to your daily routine. If daily is too much commitment, commit to exercising at least 3-4 times a week.

When I first started running in the morning, I hated it. The first week of running was miserable. Every time I ran, I had a hard time breathing, and my feet hurt too. But rather than focus on the pain, I looked for the areas where I saw small improvements.

I noticed that after running, I had more energy throughout the day. Since I routinely run in the morning, the rest of my day was more efficient. My brain felt sharper, and I worked at a faster pace. As much as I hated running, I enjoyed being productive and so I continued to run each week.

The first week of running I maxed out at a mile a day. It was torture, but I pushed myself to keep running each morning. By the time I got to my sixth week of running, I maxed out at six miles a day. In addition to being productive, I lost weight and felt better about myself.

Once running became routine, I then focused on a new area of my life to improve. This time I worked on reducing my self-limiting beliefs. Now that I physically felt healthier, it was about mentally feeling healthier. Once I overcame my self-limiting beliefs, I moved on to the another area to improve.

This is what I mean by getting into a good flow. Start small until you feel that you've made significant progress and then move onto the next area of your life. Before you know it, you've completely given your daily routine a makeover.

Conclusion

By now, hopefully you have a strong foundation and a blueprint of how to begin turning your life around. Again, I don't claim to be an expert, but everything that I've shared with you has been from my own experience and struggles. These are life lessons I've had the pleasure and displeasure of learning.

When I was at my lowest, I often went to sleep hoping to wake up in a different life. I wished the life I was lived was a dream, and my real life awaited me somewhere else. If only there were a reset switch, like in video games. It would be great to hit reset and completely start over. I often prayed for this switch.

Instead what I got was a second chance to do things the right way, to build the kind of life I was meant to live. I don't regret the path I took. I only wished I'd started sooner. Other than that, I'm happy with the person I am today.

Now I'm sharing all my lessons with you so that you can hopefully begin turning your life around. What's done is done. Everything up until this point is considered the past. Now I want you to create a fresh blank slate for yourself and start making plans for a better tomorrow.

Keep pushing, keep fighting, and keep moving forward. I'll be here to support you every step of the way. When times get tough, think back to this book and my stories. Study the lessons that I have laid out and used it to guide your way out of the darkness.

You've got this!

Sincerely,

Hung Pham

If you enjoyed this book and want more tips and strategies on building a better life, sign up for my newsletter at: http://www.missionandpossible.com

P.S. Could you please take a minute and leave a review for this book on Amazon? Your feedback will help me continue to write Kindle books that produce positive results in your life.

P.S.S. If you enjoyed this book, I highly recommend you check out my other Amazon bestseller books on personal development.

Cheat Sheet

Don't Worry; Everybody Fails – Failure is often a necessity to become successful. Some of the greatest people in history have had to overcome their share of failures. Don't worry; you're in good company.

Change an Outcome by Changing Your Perspective – If you don't like something, then fix it. If you can't fix it, then stop complaining about it. It's not always the problem you have to solve, but rather how you react to the problem.

Live Life with Results, Not Regrets – Regrets are a natural part of life, but try not to have too many of them. Instead, create meaningful memories that can take the place of regrets.

Cats Aren't the Only Ones with Nine Lives – It takes seven years to master a skill. Starting at age 11 until the age of 88, you have eleven opportunities to be great at something. These are your lifelines.

Stop Victimizing Yourself, Stop Blaming Others – Be responsible and accountable for your actions. Blaming others doesn't solve the root of the problem; it only covers it like a Band-Aid.

Make the Most of the Time You Have Now – You can't make up for the lost. You can only make the most of whatever time you have left. Don't dwell on the past, instead, focus on creating a better tomorrow.

Stop Making Problems Bigger Than They Are – There are serious problems, and there are not so serious problems.

You don't need to magnify anything that isn't considered life-threatening. Keep it small and manageable.

Be True to Yourself and Own Who You Are – Be confident in yourself and your abilities. Everybody has flaws and insecurities. Own them like a boss and others will admire and respect you for that.

Use Your Story to Inspire Others – Everybody has a story to tell. Regardless of where you are in life, you always have an opportunity to help others by sharing your own story.

Happiness On the Inside Equals Happiness On the Outside – How you feel about yourself internally will project how you feel about others externally. Give yourself permission to be happy.

Start Small, Start Now – Turning your life around begins with making simple changes at first. You don't need any major life altering change. You just need small quick wins, and you need them now.

Change Your Environment to Change Your Life – You are the average of the five people you spend the most time with. If you're looking to do more, then seek out others who share the same goals and aspirations as you do. Find your tribe.

How a Four Letter Word Can Spark Change – Even the most successful people couldn't get to where they are without help. Don't be afraid to ask for it when you need it. Together we can achieve more.

Keep One Eye on the Past and One Eye on the Future – The struggles you overcome are a lesson about how resilient you are. Keep an eye on the past to never forget that, and one eye on the future to continue pushing forward.

Invest in Yourself for the Greatest Return Possible – You are your biggest competitive advantage and number one investment. If you want more out of life, take the time to invest in yourself to be better.

Creating a Blueprint for Success – Build healthy habits so that they naturally become a part of your daily routine. Learn to create natural highs so that your brain becomes addicted to success.

How to Begin Today – Pick one or two tips in this book and start applying them to your life. Focus on quality over quantity. Work on getting into a good flow and celebrate the small improvements.

About The Author

Hung Pham is the founder of Culture Summit, a conference that helps companies succeed through building strong cultures. Before Culture Summit, Hung spent over ten years working at several Fortune 100 companies.

In his 20's, Hung dealt with a serious gambling addiction that led to severe depression and financial debt. Through hard work and persistence, he has turned his life around and become a successful entrepreneur. You can learn how too by downloading his free 33 page eBook at www.missionandpossible.com.

Made in the USA
Middletown, DE
03 January 2024

47118011R00076